STARS AND DREAMS

STARS AND DREAMS

by

Antonio Kinchen

LIMNARIAN

Limnarian

Maryland

Limnarian

Printed in the United States of America

ISBN
978-0-9995157-0-9

Cover: "Galaxy IV" by Pauline Moss
Web site: https://paulinemoss.deviantart.com/

Web site: www.facebook.com/Limnarian

Contents

POMPEII

Tell me why the snow is true
Of warmth, and idles where it moves,
And morning looks with evening's face,
As we dream sooner than stars ray.

Heaven avow; can it be true
That billows make cries sail to you
As but a humming in Pompeii,
As we dream sooner than stars ray?

Bereft Of Requisite Wing

Pardon if the thoughts I fling
Sail young as plume-shy nestlings,
Bereft of requisite wing.

Pardon if I am a feral wind,
Urging for too bare a limb to bend,
Bereft of requisite wing.

Staring Down

Staring down,
I wish for nothing more
Than to see your shadow
Sail across the floor.
And to sense the breeze you'd birth
If you were to traverse.
And to seize from that air
Your scent it would wear.
Staring straight,
I wish to heed your love.
Or if your lips
Can't turn it to discourse,
To let their grips
Your silent love report.
I, stocked with dreams
And shy of truth,
Staring up,
Solicit God for you.

The Dreamer

For sorrow slumber served as his relief,
But as he suffers now so does repose.
He dozes yet dormancy proves so brief
He muses more alive than with eyes closed.

I walked a thin path between the trees of an infinite woodland. Keeping to a quest for which I knew no purpose, I was urged forth only by the contours of a throbbing light. A light that softened the rough skins of the earth before me. A light that always seemed just around the next turn.

Unlike myself, I had not stared down for the occasional assessment of my course, but thoughtlessly progressed, steered by a luster that made nature's blackened entities all seem of the same substance.

Finally, I faced the source. Clad partially by evening's dim air, he stayed concealed like a child hiding behind its mother. It seemed to me that he preferred to be halved by the night. As if he sought to sheath all of himself but heaven would not allow. I was certain that he was the very manifestation of sorrow, or if he wasn't, they were surely of the same blood.

With the suspended noise of the elements I crushed, a silence grew as full as the blanched air.

I began to mind my breathing, which beat for the stress of my journey. Then did I note the conduct of his aura. I measured my breaths and as I breathed so did he dispense his light.

I remember how she called me the moon.

Was it by will or error that his love
Had once compared him to the dreary moon?
This he pondered until weariness drove
The dreamer to a dream which he quit soon.

She fared swiftly, while time's celerity forsook all else. I could sense the red she wore urge fire to my chest. I could feel the potent hue skim my face, like the gentle hand of Venus roaming Adonis.

Her black seemed untouched by heaven's light, or touched, but even heaven's light was denied there.

I assumed that the chrysalis of air that begot her observed her beauty, and therefore grew reluctant to release her, and clung to no avail, and her cause for prompt proceeding was her inability to ease the momentum she'd encouraged in her escape.

Time provoked the world again as her course drew to its end. I watched her go until, like rain, she returned to the air from which she had come.

The clamor of existence resuscitated me, making me remember myself and the traffic of the street.

She passed me by as if I was as relevant as the pavement her shadow barely knew. But I knew that we were not strangers, and that we had loved each other in a time lost.

I remember how she called herself a butterfly.

The butterfly was for love departed.
And if, he thought, romance is like the rain,
Which from air does have it's being started,
Then after being goes to air again,

He wished it too like water in the sense
That it returns just as it gets it hence.

The Moon, The Sun, And The Heavens

For many mornings the moon stood early to admire the sun and the heavens. But the two did not find this to be good, for the moon might then receive some of the praise man was to give to them, rather than go unnoticed at night as commonly.

So, the heavens bestowed upon the sun a bow and arrows with which it was to shoot the moon to death at morning, and to the moon it gave a particular immunity, so that by night it would be healed, invulnerable to harm, and rise to do its work.

And so, did it occur for many cycles.

The moon grew wise to the arrangement and, feeling discouraged, quit its astral state to live as a man. This so, it's silver rondure would not be.

When the heavens learned this, it bid the sun to find and retrieve the man, lest his late duties go undone.

The sun, too, quit its astral state, becoming a mortal woman. This so, its golden rondure would not be.

At this the world was blanketed in heavy blackness. The woman had to be swift. And so, she was.

Not long after, she found the man selling bread on the side of a busy road. She prayed to heaven for guidance, to which it bade her end her counterpart no different than before, and the street merchant, dying a man, would return to his initial form.

Upon approaching him she did but shoot her arrows, to no avail.

For with the absence of her rondures radiant light it was always night now, and then he was invulnerable.

People witnessed the man's strength and began to praise him.

This so, his opposers noted that evil empowers those it should afflict.

Do You Dream?

Do you perceive the light alone
When day's avowing star has clomb,
Or do you get the rousing gleam,
And on our old acquaintance dream?

And does that light, which gilds the woods
And grants the heaven's hue to floods,
Show earthly matters as they seem,
Or do you us acquainted dream?

UNSATED

I bade a lover's pen a love confess.
I prayed " Note withdrawn love and love may dwell! "
But marked it only if it would be pressed,
As woodlands whisper but if winds compel.
I bade time on its way a time renew.
I prayed " Turn to old hours and they may fare! "
But marked it only moments coursing true,
As pitch-dark skies must only nights declare.
So, I, unsated, did the air entreat
Bidding it's king grant me lasting repose.
For unremitting sleepers nothing seek
And are not discontented for their woes.
But lulled he only mortals by days grayed,
As reapers pluck crops of the eldest age.

O, TALL RONDURE

'O, tall rondure teach me how
You do beam so truly now.'
Thus, I prayed the wintry light
That abided in the night.
Then he did his beam profess:
'By my love.', he did confess.
'For as one no light I sire,
But I shine by my love's fire.'

O, Tall Rondure II

'O, tall rondure teach me how
You do burn so truly now.'
Thus, I prayed the fiery form
That abided in the morn.
Then she did her heat profess:
'I am wintry as the rest.
For no flame do I design,
But I blaze by my love's shine.'

NARCISSUS

The black river rolls,
Bearing a silvery horn
That moistens never.

Love On

Love on
For fairest moments fare in haste,
While those unfair do ever seem embraced.

Love on
So I may sense than dream some bliss,
Not frequenting such things in somnolence.

Love on
For Eden's first did prove to heaven
Per lonely soul another should be given.

A Thousand Dreams

Thou lovely nest
About thee rest
A thousand dreams
Of pass'nate stares
And palms in pairs
And hearts that for hearts flame.
Of prayers given
To the highest heaven
Ne'er for the composer
But rather winged
For what pertained
To favoring a lover.
Though with no fault
In sight thou shalt
Become a weeping eyer
To find quite true
Thy bosoms view;
'Love never was a liar.'

THE LONELY POET

Prithee, knight-at-arms,
Profess thy sires heart
Which didst bestow thee in such woeful art.

'Learn'd he a woman's charms.
Therefore, affliction be
For vassals, vanquishers and sovereignty.'

Prithee, unfold him
Who gave lonely wars to ye,
Where lover is both friend and enemy.

'Schem'd he for a woman's whim.
Therefore, admirers haunt
Silver hills and crowns of flowers flaunt.'

ECHO

Were admirers pools,
I would all thy dreams inform,
Aureate flower.

Ace And The Spider

Y'ain't never heard of Darren T. Adams?! Corporal Adams?! Darren Divine?! A-Bomb Tom?! Ole Ace?! Seriously?! Fought in World War II. Took out twenty-five Italians one night, but only twenty-five cause the leftovers offed themselves. Master-Hunter Darren Adams?! Prolly made sport of the hydra and drove dragons to extinction. Never?! Alright. Y'ain't hip so I'll clue ya.

Darren T. Adams, we'll call 'em Ace for times' sake, was born in '22. Enlisted in '41, at the green age of 19. Joined up pretty young, considerin' the affair. Still shocked y'ain't heard of 'em.

Anyways, still had milk 'round his mouth but was just as good as them other fellas. Better even.

After the war, he tried his hand at actin', but that, that was too tame for ole Ace. Prolly wasn't no good at it no how.

He still dreamed of drawin' blood. So, he took to huntin'. Now this was intimate turf, 'cause he done it as a youngin' with his pa, Ben. Prolly what drew him to the army in the first place. Ya know? Kill punks for free.

He was bloodthirsty ever. Heck, the stories don't mention his ma, now that I think of it. Prolly killed ole Grace first thing, on the way out and all.

Ace was a stone-cold killer. Wasn't a beast on this wide Earth he couldn't bag. Grizzlies, whales, Japs; no sweat. Yep. Not a soul he couldn't clip. But there's a tale of once, when no matter how hard he tried there was one critter he just couldn't crush.

A spider.

I know. I know. A big tickle. You're prolly done with ole Ace right about now, huh? Hunter-soldier Ace Adams bested by some bug? Nuts; I know, but hear me out.

So, Ace, as I said, could bag anything. Alright? N-E-**THANG**. But one afternoon, just boozin' in his room, he stared up and saw a spider strung a wire from one side of the ceilin' to another. Cornerwise.

Now this was a hefty wire. Not one of those you have to squint for. He saw it just billowin' like hairs from gramma's brush. But just as quick as he caught sight of it he found that critter strollin' 'cross, passin' his cot, makin' its way to the closet.

Now Ace knew better than to lose it in there. And as brave as he was he hated him some spiders. Wasn't so much scared. They just sorta grossed him out. Didn't want to think it was crawlin' 'round in every pair of trousers he put on, or, or 'neath the collar of every shirt.

So, no later than he cast an eye on it, he flat out bobbed that wire. Then he combed every inch of carpet near his closet, trustin' that's where the meddler fell. Well, with it bein' so small, dust-brown, blending with everything; Ace lost him. Needle in a haystack sorta deal.

He saw a batch of webs right over the closet. Same corner the spider was workin' toward. Ace knew it was in there now. Or maybe that's what the lil' devil wanted him to think. But he had to be sure so Ace combed through the closet. Didn't find the spider, webs, nothin'.

'Course that bugged him real good. Ole Ace wasn't much versed in failin'. Cheered himself up with a touch of his handy headboard whiskey and piled Z's. Or tried to. Barely slept a wink. Every tickle and itch had him jumpin' to catch that critter on him. But it was just his dog, Jack, wrigglin' in the cot.

If Jack flinched, huffed, or cracked one Ace woke up thinkin' it was the spider. And he'd sip from his headboard stash and snooze. And woke and sipped and woke and sipped for all Jack's squirmin'.

Only way that bottle left its spot is when he sipped or swapped it for a new one. Ace never threw it out for bein' wide open all the time, or, or lived-in, or nothin'. That man drank more than he ate.

Next mornin' he woke and saw fresh webs in a different corner. So, Ace knew that germ was still kickin'. You gotta think that embarrassed the poor fella. This big, bad, alpha male, undone by a flea.

Ace was never gonna catch that blasted thing and paranoia started to bug him more than the bug did, so he just stopped carin'. And that very night he slept like a boulder. Jack could'a been gnawin' his leg off and he wasn't gonna budge. Ace didn't wake and he didn't sip.

Next mornin' he felt good. Real good. Hadn't slept that sound in a long while. Decided it was time to turn over a new leaf. Decided to quit drinkin'. So, after he tossed on some fresh threads, carefree, he grabbed his bottle to bid farewell, and when he did he found somethin'.

Dry and curled up and tucked in the corner of his headboard he found the spider. That first night he saw him he crushed him with his bottle when he went for a pick-me-up. The webs in the corner that he thought was new, those was old. He just ain't pay no mind 'til the day he saw 'em.

The moment he gave up he got what he wanted.

Ended up celebrating with a drink. And then another, and another, and another after that one.

Drank himself to sleep.

Forever.

REMEMBRANCE

Behold, lover mine,
our eyes upon us beaming
reveal lovers love ere time;
now is but for lovers dreaming.

The Lady Of The Meadows

With much obeisance, fiery threads
curtsy as the stallion treads.
Perchance a steed in ambling state
is all to rule her tawny pate.
A man-at-arms nor that man's lord
may this celestial's dreams afford.
Undoubtedly her features sway
her witnesses to haunt her way.
I therefore sometimes survey left
trusting such flocks follow abaft;
neglecting that the lonely mead
is where but three of us proceed.
Then I behold the present twain;
my horse and then the sprite again.
Yet scarcely note the sable beast
beneath the nymph of brilliance vast.
I held him at a brother's cost
yet now so as a stranger lost.

Mine eyes fly o'er him in haste
to perch upon her star-like face.
Lo! Flowers ne'er did last in flame
as those that on her garland hang.
Nor metals ever shine so true
as mine own mirroring her hue.
Nor nothing drape the arid globe
as the full fuchsia of her robe.
Nor doth a carrot nor a peach
bear the rich coral of her cheeks
Lo! Pendulous her unshod feet;
pure as snow earth ne'er did meet.
Amidst the scent of bergamot
ne'er shall departure strike my thought.
Keep her my horse, I'll keep his rib,
awaiting her to secrets give.
Her reticence, eterne or brief,
ne'er shall dissuade my firm belief.
O, firmly so, I do believe
my love was hers ere earth was treed.
Ere it was whelmed. Ere heaven starred.
Ere that realm black or with a god.

The Witness

Idle waters
glisten less
than those alive.

When A Mountain Buds

Chapter 1

The cacophony of customers ceased. The coins had run their marathon. The counter quit its commentary. The bills cut their applause.

The printer squealed, spewing sheet after sheet. The sound was all to span the building.

I kept the cash room in silence. The peace prompted productivity and indolence.

I yawned, curving clockwise to pluck my phone from my pocket. I steered its face to mine like a woman checking her makeup mirror. The gesture woke the slab's display.

The screen faded from black. The animation was swift, but, for a worn and curious man, served as a sluggish share of unwelcomed suspense. Its wallpaper gleamed like a firefly in the night. The force of its light was jolting. A teal ocean glazed my eyes, flaunting foamy water, like a marine mosh pit. Water. Water and nothing more. Though a thrilling sight, this unattended sea was not my wish.

He hadn't sent a word. Not the customary "Need a ride" or the alternative "What time you get off" (, which, in essence, implied the former). It was strange. Very strange, but a strangeness I approved. I knew I'd be longer, and I didn't need him nagging for the wait.

I hate being rushed, and if my older brother was a superhero then, screaming and rushing would've been his powers. I would've rather spent twenty dollars on a cab than get the incessant "Have you left yet". *That* than catch the sermon that succeeded the shutting of his passenger door. *That* over listening to a second of failed subtle sarcasm. That night I would take my time, and literally pay the price.

Ray always had a thin temper. Always. I remembered the stories. One told of how he'd scratched our then infant sister. Another of how he'd spark at boys who liked her too, too much.

I remembered the pictures. The pictures of little, red-haired Ray, which was itself eerie, since the rest of us were black-haired. The pictures of him running in boots of blur or those of his arms pretzeled. His brows were ever bent like the sun lived on them. I'd dream through the pictures thinking "This kid's trouble".

Ray was the eldest, and more than a decade my senior. I had decided that his fiery disposition was simply the product of novice parenting. He was the first pancake, and those never come out right. Ray was mice on a minefield; a tantrum in a microwave; Vesuvius with legs; just waiting to blow.

I was accustomed to it. We all were. Consequently, we'd avoid him, as best we could. Surely, it was at least what *I* did.

It was a fine day. Not exceptional. Just fine. No complications at work, technical or human. No scrape with the girlfriend. Nothing. Just a crawling, quiet Wednesday.

My phone groaned. I drew it with no urgency. I didn't care about missing the call. My family and friends knew better than to bother me while I was working, and anyone else could just leave a voicemail.

301 235 - 3514

It was my father's job. The first six digits gave it away. Normally he'd appear as a contact, but his building had so many numbers I hadn't saved them all.

"Hello."

The breath was backed by a bogus bliss, but the simplicity of the salutation spoke my true sentiment.

My word was miraculous. Most nights I'd miss my father's calls by will, because he'd "umbilicalized" my phone.

From behind the glass poured a different voice. It was coarse and tired.

I should've known it wasn't him, but my selfish brain was stubborn. My father's work schedule was fixed, and I still hadn't retained it. He had been off for a few days.

The caller was a commander who had been trying to reach my father. Dad had no phone. Instead his calls came to me. When the commander sought discussion, I'd ignored him trusting he was my father.

I spun in the creaky office chair, neglecting the computer screen to favor my full attention. The commander spoke solemnly, stating only that the matter was of substantial significance. He urged to discuss it with my father immediately.

He hung up, abruptly, as if his swift stoppage would prompt my speed. It didn't. His words were sharp and thin. Their sharpness and thinness made the secret truth more daunting.

My brows mingled as I looked to the cancelled call. My eyes drank the digital expanse again, then clomb and perched upon the air. They hung there like a scarecrow's, dreaming the cryptic message.

I broke my gaze, letting the phone's blonde glow coat my face. One thumb strummed the glass as the other brushed my chin.

Raymond

In a sea of words his had drowned. Our message thread was low. We hadn't talked for days. I read his silences as if they'd shed light on the situation. They didn't. Instead they taught me of myself. I saw how I only sought Ray when I desperately needed something. I was something of a stranger to him.

I threw my head back and breathed a drawn-out breath. I stared past the missing ceiling tile, past the slanted steel skeleton and the bare tendinous wires, into some secret region of scampering thought. There, in that removed realm, I met the manifested truth, like Moses the burning bush, and it was fiery and fierce.

I focused on the phone. My thumb smeared the greasy glass.

Kenneth

I found my younger brother's thread. Likewise, I learned I scarcely sought him past necessity. The truth flared in my chest.

Tell dad to call commander brown.

Kenny was sleepless. I knew he'd respond, and promptly. And he did.

Rays in trouble.

That's all he sent. Nothing more. Maybe he knew no more. Or maybe he did but didn't want to wound my work. Maybe he rushed into action and had no time to tell the tale. I didn't know the truth, but I learned then that trouble is troubling, and secret trouble is worse.

I rubbed my face, fiercely, like a cutman ringside. I was weary and worried.

I looked to the mound of paper in the mouth of the monstrous machine. The documents required nightly auditing, but my head was lifted. I didn't care if I complied with policy.

I procured the papers like a pilgrim hushing his passengers; seated and twisting backwards. The sheets were warm. Their touch dealt a temporary ease. I convened the documents between pincer-like hands, beating their bases on the table top for their compositional uniformity. It was a useless act, for I only followed with cramming the mass into my wall-mounted bin where it inevitably fanned and flopped.

"Tomorrow" I ruled reassuringly.

My mind was far from me. I decided to leave. I returned to the computer, which by then was soundly sleeping, and woke it with a nudge of the space bar.

I'd unlocked my profile, entered my seven-digit employee number, and struck the "Clock Out" button so swiftly that the blinking cursor in the vacant text field fooled me into thinking that I hadn't done the deed at all. I'm no stenographer but my fingers found the fairly foreign keys magnetically.

I rose to meet my bin, which hung by the door. I peeled away my sooty sports watch and staple-bound nametag and wed them with the papers on the wall. I withdrew the two pens from my breast pocket, and flung them to the desk not caring if they rested there.

I stood in the doorway, scanning the room. I'd done so every night before I left. Every night since the night I forgot $500 on the counter.

All was well.

I slid through the door briskly, breezing beyond the brief hall between it and the main office. I'd reached the second room before I heard the chomp of the brawny black plate meet its frame.

I walked past the alarm system panel and whispered what it read.

"Armed and secure."

This utterance was for my surety.

I threw on my windbreaker, as if the building breathed a long and brumal breath, and then my backpack as if the jacket was the imaginary gust.

I backtracked to the panel to irrelevantly ensure that it was equipped, because not arming the safe was something I'd done before as well.

All was fine.

I exited the main office and observed its door slowly loiter to a close. I watched it shut, but the mingling metals and two-tone binding beat were not enough. I jiggled the cold handle belligerently because once I left it unlocked.

All was well.

I descended the stairs speedily, like they'd crumble at my touch. At the main level I ensured the quadruple entrance doors were secure, yanking the polished pull handles as if I sought to rouse them from some substantial slumber. They were locked and I knew that they were. I had locked them two hours earlier, but customarily, I'd double checked everything.

I unsheathed my phone again, seeking the cab's saved number. I paced to the middle of the lobby, as if there the cellular signal was strongest. In place I placed the call.

The conversation was crisp and direct. Acutely business-like. A trend that night. At its conclusion, I went downstairs.

I left the building through the lower level exit. The door only opened one way. That route prevented me from unlocking one of the upper level quartet, only to lock it again from its base on the other side. The course would not require that I kneel with my back to the world, and that, coupled with my obscuring windbreaker, made me look like an average joe and not the owner of a business, ripe for robbery.

An escalator led from there to the plaza. It was powered down. This was often the case when it was late. I sprinted up the metal stairs, sensing their harshness through the soles of my worn work shoes.

I slowly reached the short peak. My effortlessly earned fatigue was saddening. I recalled how during college I'd divinely ascend the escalator from the train station, which was at least four times as high, five days a week.

The modern ziggurat led me to my building's front. I'd taken a trip hellward and up the sleeping teeth to exceed a door that I initially faced.

By now it was drizzling. Ambidextrously, I applied the hood of my jacket. I walked across the plaza toward the school on 15th St., where the driver would wait. I hugged the library then, because I knew walking the plaza's right meant mingling with the homeless.

I hummed boldy so that no bystander sensed my fear. Fear, I thought, drew crooks, while fearlessness repelled them. I stopped at the curb, smoothly scanning before crossing the sleepy street. Smoothly, to further accentuate my fearlessness.

I stood at the school's front. Its glass doors haloed me with a sharp and static light. That way I'd be visible for the driver. The school's facade also featured a canopy that shielded me from the rain. As a manager it was my job to make smart moves. The strategy behind my waiting place tickled my ego.

I watched the vagrants pace behind the street. They mumbled nonsense. They were so alive, as if they didn't know that the night is when the living sleep.

I gave the school's address because giving my job's meant the drivers would never find me. It was often they'd start small talk, asking what was seemingly the obvious;

"Leaving school?"

I'd respond mechanically;

"No. I work across the street, but if I give my job's address it sends you guys in circles."

Polite of me, for I'd refrain from bluntly confessing the truth;

"If I give my job's address you guys get lost."

I guess it was fair for them to figure that I was a student. I was a youthful looking man at a school with a backpack.

The driver must've been close because I waited no more than three minutes. He pulled up on the opposite side of the street. It was slightly disappointing. I'd given him the school's address but, *then* he stopped at my job.

He made a slight U-turn, to meet me where I stood. His tires popped pebbles and trilled water. Through the scantly lit sedan I saw the long white sleeves of his shirt dance for his hand-over-hand technique.

I parted the stridulate door, settling behind the passenger seat. I'd sit there purposely so the drivers could see me. I wanted them to feel safe.

"Thank you"

Courteously I addressed him before the door could close. I'd always done so, taking pride in treating people like people, and not like wooden servants. Not like the snobbish customers at work did.

He disregarded my words.

"Where you headed?" he asked aridly.

"Stockpoint, Maryland. 2316 Peele Dr." I replied pristinely.

He was too busy minding the map on his phone to speak.

We were in Virginia, and it was late. I watched his face's rear to read his inevitable disgust. It masked him boldly, like a clown's nose. His reluctant approval of the trip was solely signified by a silent departure.

When A Mountain Buds

Chapter 2

"Here good?"

The driver sighed the statement crisply, as the car came smoothly to a stop. His question killed my drifting thoughts. My eyes rushed to the rearview mirror. There his own hung beneath his standing eyebrows, anxiously awaiting an answer. That was the first time I'd REALLY looked at him.

He was an older man. Dust brown hair. Fat framed plastic glasses. His ivory face looked like a melted candle. Wrinkled and resolved.

Despite his sharp displeasure, I responded politely.

"Yeah; here's fine."

It wasn't. He'd already passed my apartment. I just didn't want to rile him.

"Thank you".

I left him with the words I met him with. They were more unloved then than they were with their first flight.

I exited the car, scanning the seat as the door slowly shut. Its parting awoke an inward light, making my assessment simple. I had to be sure I left nothing. I'd done so once, leaving a loaded commuter card on a bus.

I kept the sidewalk briefly, then took a shortcut through the trees. Heavy with rain, they hung like gargoyles. Thick and calm. Their silences were broken by their dripping embroidery.

It rained during the ride, but I was too fixed on my feelings to notice. I hadn't fallen asleep as I often do during long trips. Instead, I wandered beyond the glass. Awake but away. Mentally departed. My mind summoned no sight of waters blurring buildings. It kept no song of the wind-pale pearls pelting the jalopy's physique.

The moon's glacial sighs awoke my weary head, and stained the grass a ghostly green. The silver air and beans of water roosted upon the land with a symbiotic marriage. Though the trees stood in numbers, I could hear the Earth's vacancy. The world was so somber it was as if it learned the news I had yet to collect.

There was no noise of tenants, nor did they drape the steps. There were no children running the lawn bald. No cycloptic squirrels spied me sideways. Nothing. Like Armageddon was loosed and leashed while I had worked.

I scaled the stairs slowly, fearing what stories resided. I tread softly as if the minutest sound would wake the tenants.

I paused at my pumpkin-green door, and palmed the cold knob lightly like it was the forehead of a dying child. I paused again, prolonging my approach. Behind a deep breath I turned the sphere methodically like a baker kneading dough. I paused, praising the silent maneuver, then palely pushed forward.

The hinges screeched sharply as I divorced the vile form from its frame. The door thumped considerably though I shut it with the purest precision. I fastened its dual locks, which chimed in on the clamorous composition.

I crossed the dark living room so subtly you would have sworn I soared. Not clashing with the shaded furniture was a miracle. I was certain, though, that the door and its components had alerted someone.

I reached the end of the hall which, unlike the living room, was lit. Its light was ever burning to favor travel to the first room. This was more so for dad, who'd come home late enough to need it.

The whisper of brass beckoned my ear. The door before me bid farewell to the cavity it kept with a clingy kiss. My mother quit her room mechanically, bearing the black aluminum bat she kept for nights when she was home alone. She stood partially in the doorway, her back perched against the frame.

She wore the sternest face with a subdermal look of dismay. It was as if she was dreaming and her eyes didn't get the memo.

She had yet to speak, but she didn't have to. Her features spoke volumes. I doubt ever seeing such a look on her before. She was like a painting of an afflicted soul. Conquered. Breathless.

If ever she wore such a face, it was in time so removed that I can't remember. I'm sure there was a match when grandma passed, but I only remember the constant crying. I remember the tears and the way she dispensed them while on the floor. She was so stung that she sought embrace from dad, which was rare. The simple seeming face she kept was more foreboding than the ancient tears, her fallen form, or her figure helplessly entangled in my father's. It was more frightening than all of that.

I refrained from speaking. I knew that she had much to share and I didn't want to halt her revelation. Or maybe I didn't know what to say. Maybe she stood mutely because she didn't want her news to be true, and to my superstitious mother speaking ill drove it.

Finally, I inquired, avoiding unfavorable terms like "What's wrong?". I instead austerely breathed "What's up?".

"Ray... Ray was hit...by a car..." She spoke the words with her mind far from her, as if just then she had witnessed the event. She paused as if she'd seen enough.

I watched her with my brows mingling, feeling more pain for her pain than Ray's. I was tempted to speak. Tempted to say something reassuring. Tempted to serve some irrefutable plum of poetic wisdom. But I was speechless. And I knew that her thoughts were rich and eager.

"He was at work,... patrolling... in one of those... flimsy... golf cart... things... Someone... sped his way, and... jumped the curb and..." She paused, rubbing her neck as if it knotted. As if she too had fallen victim to the force.

Shyly, I asked for the extent of the damage. Shyly because I didn't want to learn that Ray had been paralyzed or amputated.

She confessed that aside from some cuts and bruises, he'd broken his leg.

That was all. He was still alive, and he was going to stay that way.

It's curious. Curious how any score of harm is counted kindly when it could've instead been certain death.

We kept the hall, employing silence more than words. She may have said more. Eventually. I don't recall. I was focused on retreat. And sure enough, as slick and sly as night's ink quits its post, did I depart.

I shut my door so gently it coerced no sound; like melting ice grazing melting ice. I roamed the room, conjuring reasons to blame myself. Maybe he only worked that shift for me. To pay back some debt I'd forgotten. Or to recover from the flatscreen he bought me. Maybe it was for all the gas he burned picking me up. Or maybe it was to distract himself from how lonely I'd left him.

I tried to envision the event; fathom its weight, as if experience would afford me the foul effects I felt I earned.

I drew my phone to consult the web for statistics on car accidents.

1 in 4292

That was the chance of someone being struck by a car. That number wasn't small enough, but only because now it represented Ray.

I considered that those who learn misfortune secondhand, without personal investment, that group that I was once a part of, can never truly know the pain. Were it any other person, the extent of my interest would be articulated with a desensitized "Wow. That sucks."

My back topped the blanket like a visitor in a borrowed bed. I stared past the ceiling. The silence and vacancy urged my contemplation. I thought of the event's effects on me. I feared what responsibility would recruit me. I wondered if the family would not deem my reaction strong enough. I thought and thought till thought was stopped by dreams.

When A Mountain Buds

Chapter 3

Tardily I peeled my eyes. Though the air was pale and mild, it seemed strong for succeeding the shadow of dreams.

My neck ascended, showing that I'd slept in my uniform. The tragic thoughts still ran so thick that my heart couldn't tell the previous night from that very moment. Only did my sober eyes duly discern the morning by the ivory air that crossed my open blinds. The light did commonly instill some ease in me but was powerless then.

Words dabbed my door. The voices were muffled but their tones proved their purpose. Mom spoke frantically. Dad raced to keep up.

Mom was notorious for approaching matters as if her passionate winds would solve them. She'd often spar with dad about topics in which she had no influence. It was a nuisance.

I tried my best to ignore them. I couldn't.

I remained reclined to keep them from prodding my brooding heart. Remained reclined to keep them from awakening fresh memories of grief. Remained reclined so that they would not know my mind and aim to tame it.

Despite that desire, I still had work. Responsibly, I quite my solitude.

I snuck to the shower undetected. The period of cleansing cleared my mind. The issue faded until the water stopped running. The silence was too inviting. I heard their voices again. It was like they hadn't finished or like they paused for my sake. Then, to my surprise, I caught a different voice. My sister's.

We could never get Shawn over so early, even when it was planned. I soon learned that she'd come because they were going to visit Ray at the hospital.

I exited the bathroom as covertly as I found it, and evaded Shawn for the same reasons I did my parents. I began to feel cruel knowing that I wasn't going with them. Ray was conscious then so he would know that I was absent.

I considered informing the other managers, but I didn't want to trouble them. I acknowledged then that I was disregarding Ray's feelings in favor of others.

A big part of me wanted to work. At the hospital I'd feel useless. I feared finding him flat like furniture. I feared frequenting a place with souls sitting solid as rocks. Rocks, erupting red, hot despair.

A knock animated my door. Behind a mild pause I granted access.

"Yes?"

Kenny entered, revealing that he'd forsook his laidback look in favor of a suit. Still, he donned that stupid hat.

I can't recall how our conversation began, but of course it led to talk of Ray. He told me that Ray's story was featured on the news, and that Ray asked him to deliver a hug to me. So, we hugged, then Kenny returned me to solitude.

It was awkward. We hadn't hugged often. In fact, I couldn't remember the last time we did.

I explored the same mystery in regards to Ray. I'd hugged him years prior when his temper won him permanent vacation from home. Then I realized that, generally, I never acknowledged my family's worth. I began to fear missing the opportunity.

You hear that sort of thing all the time; acting before it's too late. When it came to Ray and I "too late" had been too close.

I walked toward my bed, kneeling to grab my computer from underneath. There is where I stored it, still in its original packaging.

I sat, setting the box before me. The sturdy mattress squeaked. I unpacked the massive machine and mounted it upon the case. Once it awoke I navigated to the news site.

Ray's incident still hung on the home page. He was something of a celebrity but for reasons so tragic and crippling he couldn't relish his fame.

Seeing the report fueled my fear. The image of the tattered cars was torture. I hadn't dreamed them so deformed.

The reporters sold the crash as fatal for both parties. Reading the article, you'd think that Ray was dying or dead. Maybe they truly trusted such, or maybe they simply sought to spice the story up.

I seethed, suspecting that to them the wreck was beneficial. They didn't care for my brother at all, just the publicity. I grew angry. Angry at the reporters, the camera crew, the network. Even the viewers who'd regard the case with a desensitized "Wow. That sucks."

Ray's assaulter was comatose. That's all I knew of him. No name. No reason. Nothing. As wrong as it was, I never felt sorry for him. He was guilty, and he wasn't my brother. What I did consider was that in the same way I discounted the villain, the world was discounting the victim. That fact spurred my anger, and fanned the flames of my sorrow.

Shawn eventually appeared. I must've been too engrossed in the article or my feelings to hear her knock. I hadn't seen her so much. She'd lived in North Carolina a while after getting married, and when she moved back to Maryland our work schedules never agreed. Hurdles or none, we were strangers too, and I was too selfish to fix that.

Not seeing someone daily lets you simply spot the shifts in their shape. Shawn was a mother of two. She was no longer the scrawny adolescent of my youth. The armature that dubbed her "Bones" in high school was plastered with labor's relics. She wore around her eyes the ever-present weakness of mothers. Despite that, or our prevailing predicament, she met me with an honest smile. I supposed her joy to finally see me subdued the hovering heartache.

Our talk wasn't about Ray at all. Instead we toured each other's lives. My nephew, Gerald, had started school. Kindergarten. Naturally, she took pictures.

His sky-blue polo burrowed into his navy pants, leaving his little black belt bare. I'd never seen him look so efficient. But Jerry couldn't fool me. His goofy, golden mug gave him away.

He was thrilled. I could sense his eagerness through his grip on his lunchbox. In the remaining pictures his sister posed beside him. Keen for her brother's keenness, she sought school too, but Kay was much too young.

The pictures had something in common. The children's heads were wrapped in smiles. They wore them like they wore their eyebrows; boldly and incessantly.

Their lively looks were not the first I'd seen, but the most powerful. Their contentment was contagious. My lips stretched autonomously. The two were my remedy.

Shawn left, closing my door. My grin had grown no more but hadn't shrunk either. I couldn't clear it, and I didn't want to. Being met, as opposed to my suspicion, was therapeutic. Maybe it was the distracting aspect of it. Or maybe mingling with those who were involved in the same hardship but kept calm was motivating.

I thought of Ray. He needed what I had just lived. I'd see him when they visited again.

WHEN A MOUNTAIN BUDS

Chapter 4

The radio was tuneless. The tires seemed to snort the asphalt. Without doubt, I knew that I alone marked the terrestrial music. Dad drove attentively. Though I behold only the back of his head, I sensed its solemn front. Mom sat mutely. I watched her swimming eyeball watch the world. Kenny pantomimed grotesquely with flashy headphones haloing his head. The smothered K-Pop thundered through the vacant air.

We arrived at Ray's roughly fifteen minutes later. Dad artlessly acquired a parking spot. The car sighed as he wound the key from the ignition. The stillness helmed an honest silence. I quit the backseat and stood starring at Ray's building. I imagined him immured alone, marooned with only his troublesome thoughts, as I had lately been. The trio walked past me and their ambling blurs broke my trance.

The building's lobby was secured by four glass doors. Between the pairs an intercom system protruded from the wall. A simple screen and keypad granted the search of tenants by unit number.

I approached the machine. My finger fluttered before the buttons. My hand was bolder than my brain.

"A - 725"

Kenny blurted boldly.

Despite Ray's many pleas I had yet to visit him. I barely knew his building's address; only its location from a backseat. A familiar feeling filled me. Shame.

Behind a cold pause Ray's muffled voice took flight.

"Hello?"

Upon his breath I found that I hadn't heard him in months. We'd only ever texted and that, thanks to me, was sparingly. Dad intervened.

"It's your family son."

A sharp snap was Rays reply. It was the sound of the second set of doors unlocking.

We crossed the empty lobby. The floor was tiled with beige linoleum. It was worn, flashing a ghost of its old gloss. The space was blank like a sleeping hospital. The screeches of our shoes roused the room.

We boarded an elevator. In silence we ascended, consorting with only our thoughts. We were so self-centered we'd practically rode the lift alone. My stomach writhed as if a ferret was hosting a nightmare in it. I was nervous, and though I had no proof, I knew I was the only one who felt the feeling.

The walk was as wordless as the way up. Ray's door was unlocked. We entered palely. His living room was modest and clean. A cleanliness unlike the Ray I remembered. He waited speechless in a wheelchair. The rig of pristine steel and virginal nylon made his circumstance seem worse.

I caught sight of the cast on his left leg. Its presence overpowered the presence of the floating chair.

His shorts were pale and parched. His t-shirt was spent. His cinnamon skin poured from the garment's mouths. His arms and legs were scraped. Their soreness was discernable. I could feel the breached flesh breathing. I could sense the stuffy air agitating the tender sites.

Ray was daubed in bruises, as if death's desire for him was powerful, but halted before its fulfillment. The blood had in those spots built as if urgently awaiting its chance to pour. The purple patches made the transpired event still seem pending. The skin atop them beamed lustrously as if the lesser wounds sought, in a mulberry tone, to compete with the grander ones.

His broken leg was coffined in black fiberglass. I imagined that beneath the cast the fabrics of flesh that should hide subdermally were visible and stretched to unnatural extents. I trusted that the pain he hosted was like God; invisible but mighty.

He greeted the others at once, then acknowledged me singly.

"Hey brother."

He spoke the last word with a subtle stress. The accentuation meant more than it seemed. It was a commemoration of kinship. An acknowledgement of affection. But it rung most as reminder of a responsibility.

The space was strange, so I drew closer to him. His arms ascended. Their flight was alien. The appendages had a curiosity about them. I paused only long enough to mark their oddity, then met them alike. I was nervous, as if I should have rehearsed the maneuver. It lasted maybe six seconds but felt like six hours. Only our hands hiking over hills of cotton were heard. I grew more nervous. I defied the feeling by forming a question as I retreated.

"Hey. How you feeling?"

The statement spilled obligatorily. It was a silly question considering the circumstances.

"Shorter."

He answered with a subtle grin. His sparked mine.

"I've been wanting to see you."

My smile shrunk as my guilt bloomed. I realized that every moment Ray laid alive and alone in that hospital bed had to be excruciating. He wasn't married or dating. There was no woman awaiting his return. No family craving his company. And thanks to my negligence he'd been hospitalized for two days without anyone's knowledge.

I hadn't heard what he said after that. Instead I focused on his animated lips. They waved gracefully as if applauding his breathes. I stalked his sailing eyes. The copper orbs bathed in lingering light as if they clutched an ancient love. I cherished his upright structure. Though the back of his chair supported such, he'd sometimes lean forward, asserting his freedom. These were the traits of a living thing. They prompted me trim my pity.

I attended his words again when I found them flowing with tears. The waters, like commas or periods, littered his report.

It was late. The D.C. lights crammed the dim air like compound constellations. Ray traced the garden's edge, studying the abstract sculptures, which stood like stealthy demons beneath synthetic stars. His watch was careful. His foot friended the cart's brakes often. He'd been at it for hours and his bottom grew tender. He speculated stopping and stepping out for a stretch but something changed his mind. He freed the brake and for a distant humming recovered it again.

He heard an engine's howl and the infernal screech of tires. His neck twirled toward the tone where he seized the sight of a black SUV mowing down lampposts. The garish headlights of the galloping car consumed his scope and then the unsolicited and stunning embrace of metal drank his body. The short cart jerked. His leg crumbled. He was slave to the momentum, being spit from the cart's core like a famished frog's tongue.

I imagined Ray floating, seeming neither man nor deity. Resting, seeming hollow and unreal. Blooming, like a child's plastic cup, that by a callow recklessness was spilled.

He eyed the charcoal heaven as he'd soon spy the ER's celestial ceiling. Eventually he turned to his aggressor. The car exhaled a heavy haze. Ray heard the shrill songs of sirens and the familiar fuss of flying engines.

He watched as the driver was warily strummed from the scorching car by paramedics friended by firemen. The vague wad, poor of metal, snapped with the sound of dying rain. The fires billowed like falling flags, fanning the fuel stained smoke skyward. The flames engulfed the mangled mass meticulously, leaving only the trunk and front hood visible. As the inferno flourished the puffs darkened and quickened. Ray rested far from the fog but could taste it nonetheless. He coughed and the tiny tremors brought him tremendous pain. The smoke was infinite, dwarfing the fire. The sable sky hung housing the hideous cloud. The static car was converted to a dancing flame.

Ray rested, unaffected by the undulating hands of the paramedics who challenged his consciousness. He instead envisioned lost time. He saw himself as a boy in a nursery. Mom came to pick him up. She was thin and bright. So youthful in seeming that she could pass for his sister. She sported an afro, bell-bottoms and a sunny smile. Mom received Ray like a wedding gift; elated. Ray saw another time misplaced. He stood taller. His body had narrowed. His breaths could be traced in the frigid wind. Dad appeared with a cat's secrecy, wrapped Ray in a long grey trench coat, and enmeshed him like a spider stealing a fly to its web. Ray caught another time. His head soared even higher. He saw himself bearing for the first time his newborn sister, feeling fuller than he'd ever felt. He didn't remember these events until the former car forced him down, and mom and dad confirmed them with astonishment. Under the naked night Ray dreamt and dreamt till dreams were stopped by sleep.

The doctors cut his clothes away. Glass kept his pockets. Days later Ray found more inside his ears. The metallic cart gifted him a crippled leg. Gifted, since if it were plastic, as some are, he'd be dead. If he left the cart to stretch, he'd be dead. And even in the tiny mint of metal the professionals claimed he should've died. Dying never seemed so easy.

Weeks passed. Ray and I spoke more and more. Initially I chalked it up to boredom. The man had been holed up for so long. But soon I saw and did inwardly confess that Ray was different. Offering services though he was stiffly seated. Avowing frequently his adoration. Speaking as slow and mild as a missionary. Ray was different and I could see it in the flatness of his face. I could hear it, snug beneath his words, blanketing his silences. Ray was different, growing kinder with each day. More calm. More patient. He was changed, like a pyramid prompting life. Like a boulder bearing flowers. Like a viper's venom varied to a quickening cure.

Though I was never fond of Ray's "powers", I pondered if, bereft them, he'd become an abridged man. Undetermined. Lacking specificity. Compromising his worth. Though his current iteration was preferred, the transition was involuntary. The cheetah I once knew, was turtling in his somber chair. That ever-wailing wolf was hush as a dog's dinner. He wasn't the same person. A new man, deserving of a new name. I wondered if he felt it. If he felt like less or more.

I was torn. Unsure of if this shift should be prized or pitied.

Let Us Journey To The Sun

Let us journey to the sun
For here the air is frigid.
Let us tread the stony earth
Though her rind is rigid.
Let us rest upon the weary tree
Though his trunk is jagged.
The sprawled plant, bereft his crown,
Shall let light flourish aground.
Shall let a fiery air unriven
Scurry from the brilliant heaven,
Free and clear of the protesting
Of a verdure skyward resting,
To us perched over his timber.
And let us scarcely remember,
Abstracted by light-rich winds,
Trials of frigid, rigid, and jagged,
Though harsh plights initially,
Rather, measure us their ends,

Which do with our dreams agree.

Sorrow Grew Two Stars

I kissed her cheek.
No joys did she perform.
None did she speak.
Were her skin not warm
I would have sworn
My love was dead.

I kissed her head.
She stared past truth.
Before her saw no walls
Nor the world beyond.
She dreamt her youth
And tragedies recalled
As if they'd freshly spawned.

I kissed her brow.
No joys did she conduct
Nor none avow.

Were she not upward posed
I'd have supposed
My love was dead.

I kissed her head.
She quit her gaze
To question why my lips
Had often drunk her features
So, I phrased
The purpose of their several sips
And great desire to greet her.

'Sorrow grew two stars
As your bright eyes grew fixed
To darkness and air.
Your grief serves as ours.
By your torment am I vexed.
Lover's troubles lovers share.
If your happiness should fare
But while my lips upon you tour
I shall kiss you till the pair
Breathe no more.'

My purpose did she heed
And to her did it breed
A happiness she breathed
And wore upon her head.

And if still she found no ease
I'd have been led to believe
My love was dead.

LIKE SNOW

Once her balmy lips inhaled my heart.
Now they but vile creatures start.
Those brims which had to my breathes clung
Now be to a ghostly legion numb.
Those pendants pink did prompt my mirth
Now swell they many a gluttonous girth.
Her lips once drank my pass'nate airs
Now engorged by rogues is the precious pair.
Those kind collectors contained life
But grant it now to base forms white.
Those lunate frames with beauty soared
But settle now within the horde.
Her summery skin's autumnal now
And maggots melt her flesh like snow.

Amidst A Hall Of Ancient Art

A thousand suns have bent
Since first my gaze did start,
Amidst a hall of ancient art,
To find your features fairer than those lent
To the fabricated faces ambient.

But before a star's descent
Did truth to me impart
That, too, your beauty thwarts
Mortal components
Along with those of paint.

Child Of Silence

Is there, perhaps,
A thing I lack
Or
A thing, instead,
I need no more?

THE STAR THAT KNEELS FROM HEAVEN

This hand of mine
Was wont to fix
The free to friends.
Now flits it like a honey bee
Who to a precious nectar bends,
If such is she.

Promptly devote thine ear
T'where now my finger flutters.
Hapless are the bashful airs
The lonely lady mutters.
Her secret sighs her heart declare.
Alas,
Tis true, tis true;
Thy love belongs to yesteryear —
No more to you.

Crowning a cloud

I did behold
How sorrowfully her neck does fold.
How woes do wed
Her breast and head.
How dreams most foul
Sway soaring souls
To trust the dreamer dead.

Attend thine eyes
T'where now this hand
That multiplied thee hies.
Tis clear, tis clear,
Lost cavalier;
Thy love returns to yesteryear.

The words she wings,
Like bare nestlings,
Do dart and fall
Concurrently;
Yearning to nest
Within thy chest
Nigh Empathy.

Give ear!
Give ear!
Fulfill the prayer
Of the star that kneels from heaven.

If thine audition is impaired,
Yet not thy vision stricken,
Then of this unarmed archer
His hollow hand heed,
That per its fearful flutter
Bears but speed.

Thither!
Thither hover!
Be volant!
Straight recover
Thy melancholy lover
From bleak and antique dreams.

WHAT'S THE WORK OF ANTS?

What's the work of ants?
If they withdraw themselves
Would the world wither?

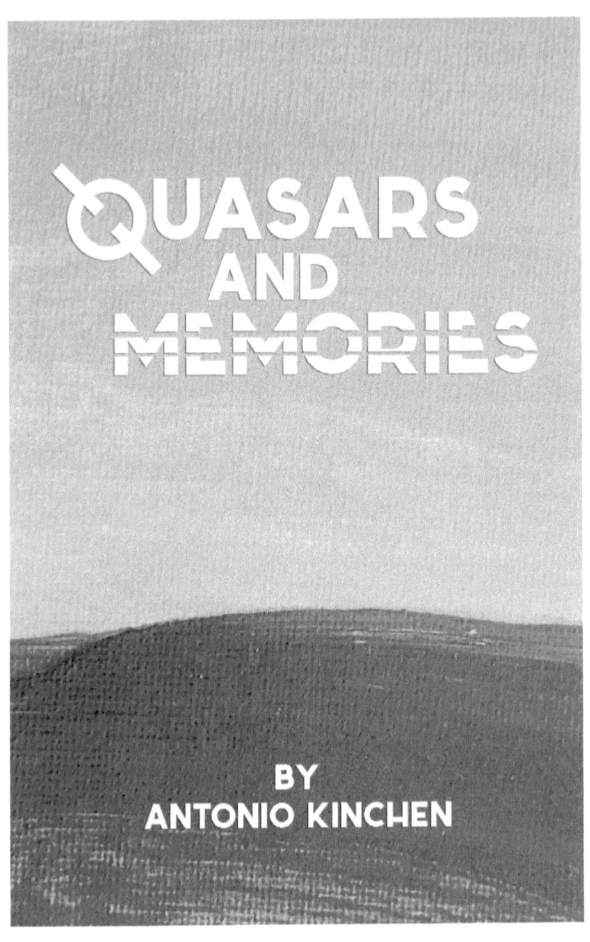

Quasars And Memories is the sequel to Antonio Kinchen's Stars And Dreams. This collection continues the evocative recounting of love learned and lost. From concise works to lengthy narrative masterpieces, experience vivid verses that breathe the truth of all hearts.

Available 2021

Follow Limnarian at:

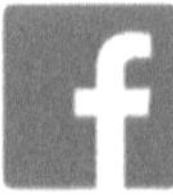

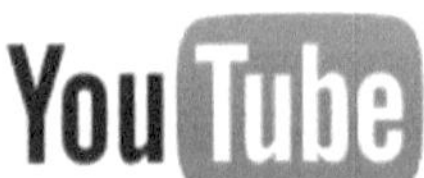

www.ingramcontent.com/pod-product-compliance
Lightning Source LLC
LaVergne TN
LVHW050938080826
845145LV00004B/1309

* 9 7 8 0 9 9 9 5 1 5 7 0 9 *